j598.864   Sabelko, Rebecca
SAB   American crows

08-11-20

CHILDREN

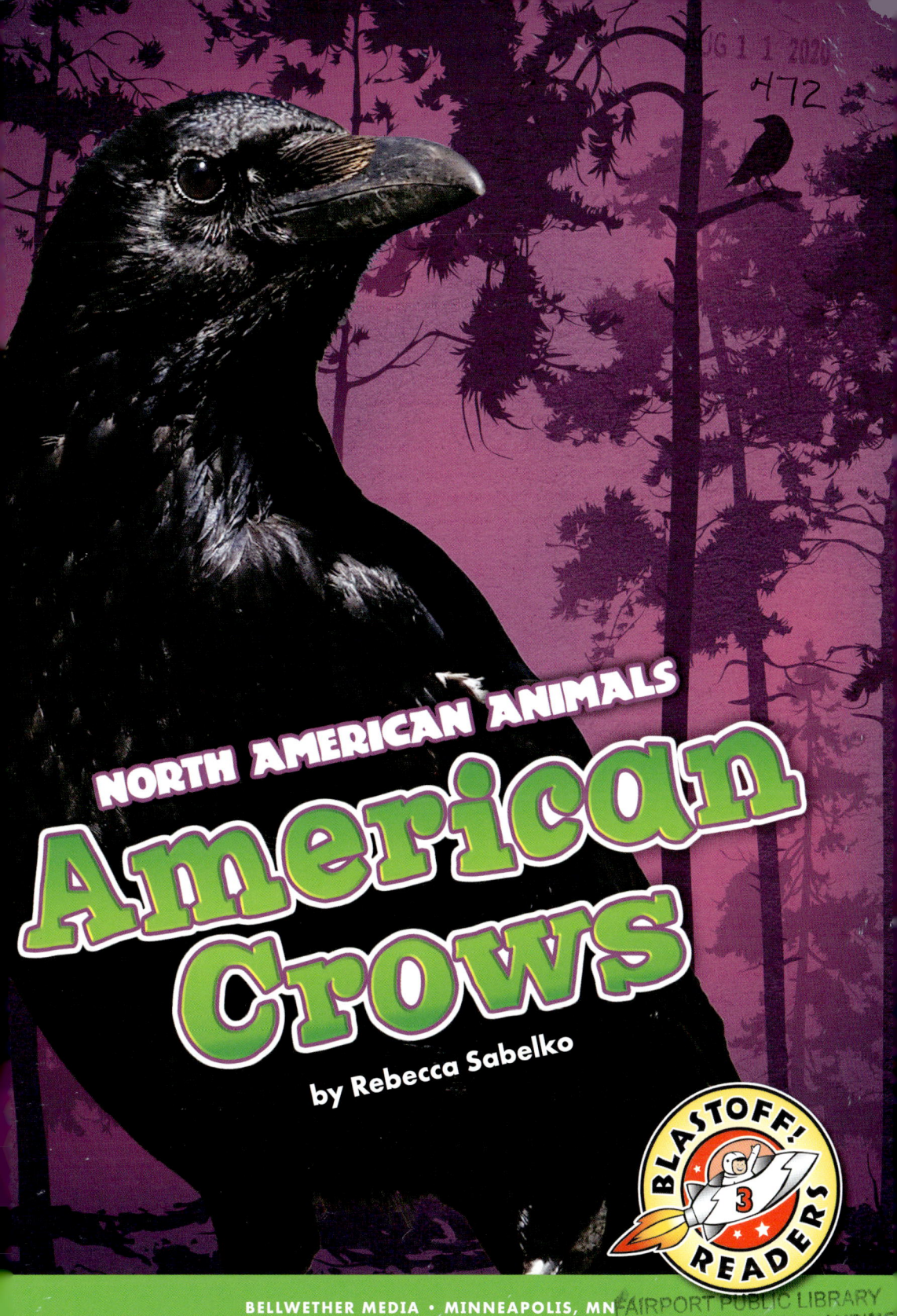

NORTH AMERICAN ANIMALS
American Crows

by Rebecca Sabelko

Note to Librarians, Teachers, and Parents:

Blastoff! Readers are carefully developed by literacy experts and combine standards-based content with developmentally appropriate text.

Level 1 provides the most support through repetition of high-frequency words, light text, predictable sentence patterns, and strong visual support.

Level 2 offers early readers a bit more challenge through varied simple sentences, increased text load, and less repetition of high-frequency words.

Level 3 advances early-fluent readers toward fluency through increased text and concept load, less reliance on visuals, longer sentences, and more literary language.

Level 4 builds reading stamina by providing more text per page, increased use of punctuation, greater variation in sentence patterns, and increasingly challenging vocabulary.

Level 5 encourages children to move from "learning to read" to "reading to learn" by providing even more text, varied writing styles, and less familiar topics.

Whichever book is right for your reader, Blastoff! Readers are the perfect books to build confidence and encourage a love of reading that will last a lifetime!

This edition first published in 2019 by Bellwether Media, Inc.

No part of this publication may be reproduced in whole or in part without written permission of the publisher. For information regarding permission, write to Bellwether Media, Inc., Attention: Permissions Department, 6012 Blue Circle Drive, Minnetonka, MN 55343.

Library of Congress Cataloging-in-Publication Data
Names: Sabelko, Rebecca, author.
Title: American Crows / by Rebecca Sabelko.
Description: Minneapolis, MN : Bellwether Media, Inc., 2019. | Series:
　Blastoff! Readers. North American Animals | Audience: Age 5-8. | Audience:
　K to Grade 3. | Includes bibliographical references and index.
Identifiers: LCCN 2018030422 (print) | LCCN 2018032517 (ebook) | ISBN
　9781681036403 (ebook) | ISBN 9781626179097 (hardcover : alk. paper)
Subjects: LCSH: Corvus brachyrhynchos–Juvenile literature.
Classification: LCC QL696.P2367 (ebook) | LCC QL696.P2367 S218 2019 (print) |
　DDC 598.8/64–dc23
LC record available at https://lccn.loc.gov/2018030422

Text copyright © 2019 by Bellwether Media, Inc. BLASTOFF! READERS and associated logos are trademarks and/or registered trademarks of Bellwether Media, Inc. SCHOLASTIC, CHILDREN'S PRESS, and associated logos are trademarks and/or registered trademarks of Scholastic Inc., 557 Broadway, New York, NY 10012.

Editor: Kate Moening　　　Designer: Josh Brink
Printed in the United States of America, North Mankato, MN.

Table of Contents

What Are American Crows?	4
Clever Crows	8
Crows of a Feather	12
Family Helpers	18
Glossary	22
To Learn More	23
Index	24

What Are American Crows?

American crows are smart and social birds. They are found in fields, forests, backyards, and city garbage dumps.

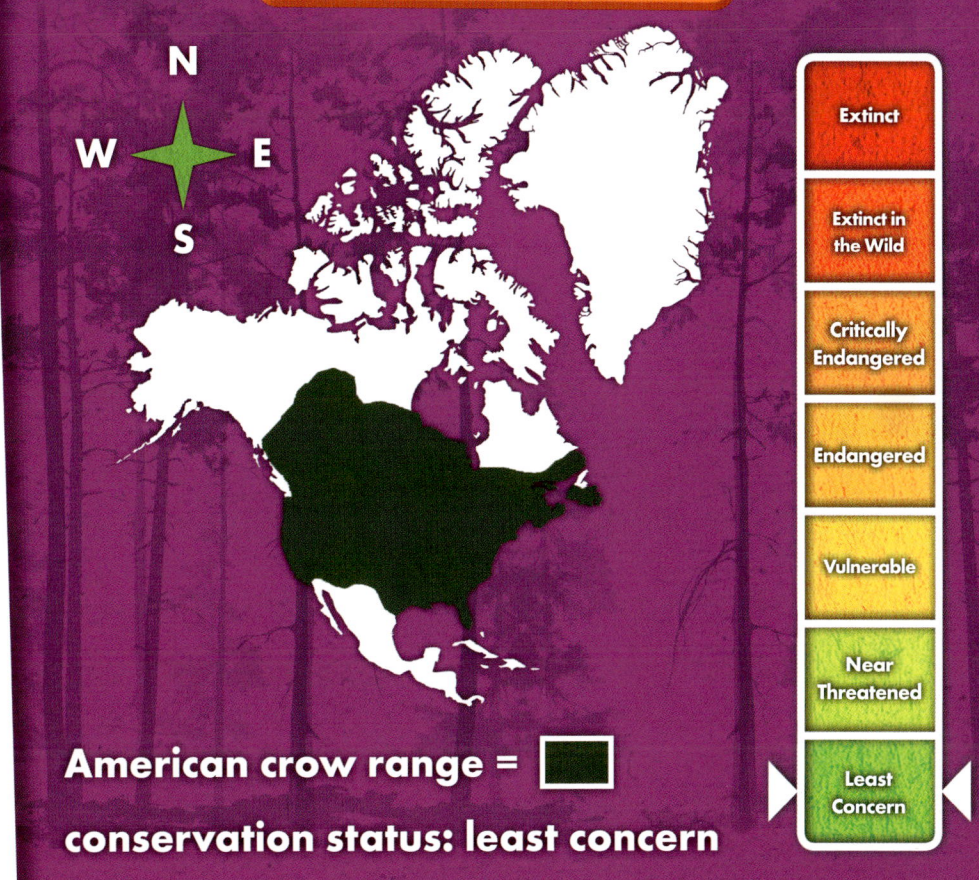

Their loud **caws** are heard throughout much of the United States. They also live in southern Canada.

Size of an American Crow

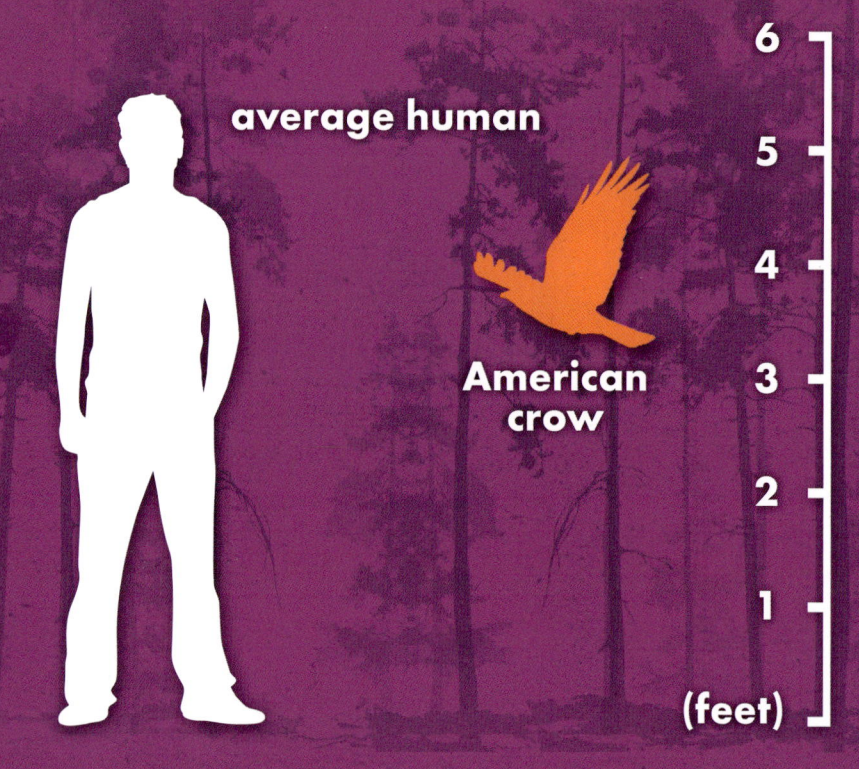

American crows have black feathers, beaks, and feet. They **molt** their shiny feathers each summer.

These birds move their rounded wings in a rowing motion to fly. They grow up to 21 inches (53 centimeters) long.

Clever Crows

American crows are **omnivores** that eat most food they find! They often make meals of seeds, nuts, and insects.

On the Menu

- June beetles
- garbage
- sparrow eggs
- sunflower seeds
- juniper berries
- earthworms

These birds feed in small groups. One or two watch for **predators** while others eat.

American crows are **aggressive** feeders. Sometimes, they chase other animals to steal food!

These birds are also smart. Some open hard-shelled food by dropping it onto hard surfaces!

Crows of a Feather

American crows live in family groups. These include a male, female, and their young. Many young crows stay with their parents for several years.

Family groups guard **territories**. They **preen** each other. They raise **hatchlings**, too.

Some American crows travel far from their family groups to join night **roosts**. These roosts give them a safe place to sleep.

Thousands of these crows gather to rest each night. Many fly back to their families when the sun rises.

Predators such as red-tailed hawks try to hunt American crows. But family groups keep the crows safe.

Animals to Avoid

raccoons

great horned owls

domestic cats

red-tailed hawks

Mobbing drives their enemies away from nests and feeding areas.

Family Helpers

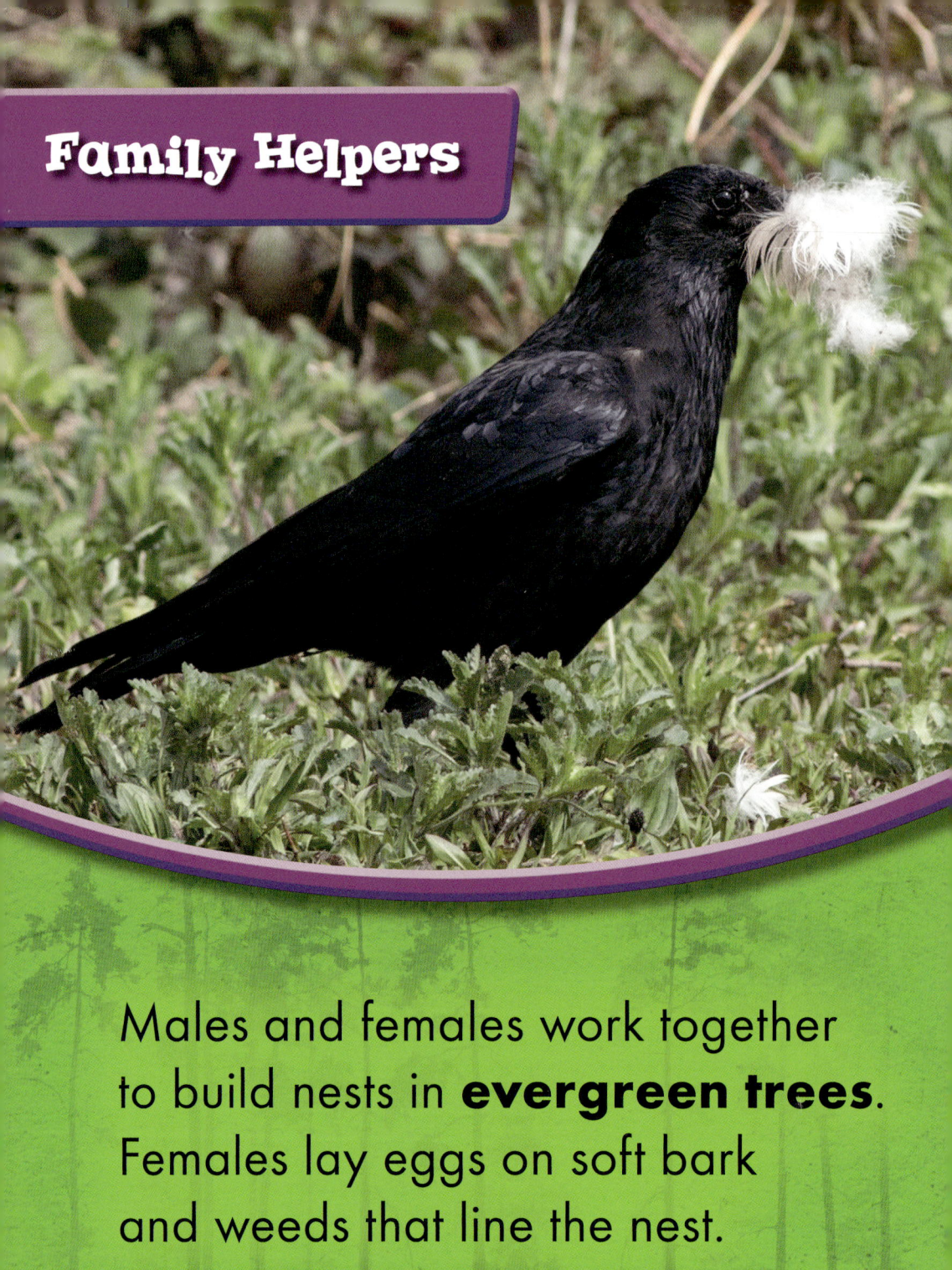

Males and females work together to build nests in **evergreen trees**. Females lay eggs on soft bark and weeds that line the nest.

Baby Facts

Name for babies:	hatchlings
Number of eggs laid:	3 to 9 eggs
Time spent inside egg:	16 to 18 days
Time spent in nest:	20 to 40 days

Soon, hatchlings break from their eggs. The family works together to feed the mother and babies.

The hatchlings grow into young crows. They help look out for their families!

Glossary

aggressive—showing a readiness to fight

caws—the loud cries of a crow

evergreen trees—trees that have leaves that stay green year round

hatchlings—baby American crows

mobbing—crowding and attacking a predator as a group

molt—to shed feathers so new ones can grow

omnivores—animals that eat both plants and animals

predators—animals that hunt other animals for food

preen—to use the beak to clean feathers

roosts—places to rest or sleep

territories—land areas where animals live

To Learn More

AT THE LIBRARY

Lajiness, Katie. *Ravens: Problem Solvers*. Minneapolis, Minn.: Abdo Pub., 2018.

Petrie, Kristin. *American Crows*. Minneapolis, Minn.: Checkerboard Library, 2015.

Rathburn, Betsy. *Blue Jays*. Minneapolis, Minn.: Bellwether Media, 2018.

ON THE WEB

FACTSURFER

Factsurfer.com gives you a safe, fun way to find more information.

1. Go to www.factsurfer.com.

2. Enter "American crows" into the search box.

3. Click the "Surf" button and select your book cover to see a list of related web sites.

Index

backyards, 4
beaks, 6, 11
Canada, 5
caws, 5
eggs, 18, 19, 20
evergreen trees, 18
family groups, 12, 13, 14, 16, 20, 21
feathers, 6
female, 12, 18
fields, 4
fly, 7, 14
food, 8, 9, 10, 11
forests, 4
garbage dumps, 4
grow, 7, 21
hatchlings, 13, 19, 20, 21
male, 12, 18
mobbing, 17
molt, 6

nests, 17, 18, 19
omnivores, 8
predators, 9, 16, 17
preen, 13
range, 5
roosts, 14, 15
size, 6, 7
status, 5
summer, 6
territories, 13
United States, 5
wings, 7

The images in this book are reproduced through the courtesy of: Edwin Butter, front cover; Cristian Gusa, pp. 4-5; hakoar, p. 7; BrianEKushner, pp. 8-9; Alekcey, p. 9 (june beetles); Only Fabrizio, p. 9 (garbage, sunflower seeds); Eric Isselee, pp. 9 (sparrow eggs), 17 (raccoons, great horned owl); Valentina Ruzumova, p. 9 (juniper berries); kzww, p. 9 (earthworms); Kevin Maskell/ Alamy, p. 10; BGSmith, p. 11 (legs, beak, full bird); Tom Franks, p. 11 (tail); sumroeng chinnapan, pp. 12-13 (sky); Richard Mittleman/ Gon2Foto/ Alamy, pp. 12-13 (birds); Robert MGouey/ Alamy, p. 13; gmc3101, pp. 14-15; PaulReeves Photography, p. 16; Chirtsova Natalia, p. 17 (domestic cats); Le Do, p. 17 (red-tailed hawk); christopher smith/ Alamy, pp. 18-19; Robert Fried/ Alamy, p. 19; photomatz, p. 20; Eugenie Robitaille, p. 21.